P9-EGN-245

TOP 10 SOCCER SUPERSTARS

BY K. C. KELLEY

Published by The Child's World®
1980 Lookout Drive • Mankato, MN 56003-1705
800-599-READ • www.childsworld.com

Photo credits:
Alamy Stock Photo: World History Archive 18;
AP Photo: Frank Augstein 4, 16; Werek/picture-
alliance/dpa 6; 8, Dreamstime.com: Dzmitry Shpak
(cover), 1; Natursports 14, 17; Steff22 15; Shao-chun
Wang 21. Newscom: Werner Baum/picture-alliance/
dpa 7; Scott Bates/Icon SMI 9; picture-alliance 10;
Frank Leonhardt 12, 13; DPP/Icon SMI 11;
Werek/PictureAlliance 19.

ISBN: 9781503827233
LCCN: 2017960465

Printed in the United States of America
PA02380

CONTENTS

Introduction: Who's Number One?. 4

Franz Beckenbauer 6

Johann Cruyff 7

Alfredo di Stefano 8

Marta. .9

Lev Yashin 10

Zinnedine Zidane 11

Diego Maradona. 12

Lionel Messi 14

Cristiano Ronaldo. 16

Pelé. .18

Your Top Ten! 20

Sports Glossary 22

Find Out More 23

Index/About the Author 24

WHO'S NUMBER ONE?

At the end of most soccer games, everyone knows who won. It's the team with the most goals! Of course, lots of soccer games end in a tie. So will there be two No. 1s at the end of this book? That's up to you!

At the end of the World Cup tournament, however, the No. 1 team is clear. It's the winner of the final game . . . and there's always a winner. So finding the top national team every four years is easy. Choosing the greatest soccer superstar of all time is a bit harder. Is it the player with the most goals? Or the player who won the most championships? Is it the top defender? Fans, experts, and fellow players all have their opinions.

Opinions are different than facts. Facts are real things. Pelé scored 1,281 goals. That's a fact. Soccer is the greatest sport in the world. That's an opinion. The goal is 8 yards wide. That's a fact. England's Wembley Stadium is the best place to watch a soccer game. That's an opinion.

Cristiano Ronaldo

NUMBERS, NUMBERS

Countries with the Most World Cup Championships

Country	
Brazil	5
Germany	4
Italy	4
Argentina	2
Uruguay	2

Some people might think soccer is not that great. (I know: Can you believe it?) But that's fine; that's their opinion. However, they can't say Pelé didn't score those goals. That's a fact. Fans in England think Wembley is No. 1. But you would find a very different opinion in lots of other world stadiums, where fans think THEIR place is No. 1.

And that's where *you* come in. You get to choose who is the biggest soccer superstar ever. You will read lots of facts and stories about these great players. Based on that, what's your opinion? Who's No. 1? There are no wrong answers about who is the best player of all time . . . but you might have some fun discussions with your soccer-loving pals! Then again, you might just pick the one with the MOST goals . . . it's up to you!

Read on, and then after you're done, make up your own Top 10 list.

The top soccer stars play for two teams. They play for money for a soccer club. That can be located in any country. They also play for their home nation against other national teams. So Cristiano Ronaldo, for example, plays for Real Madrid. He also plays for Portugal.

FRANZ BECKENBAUER

GERMANY

Franz Beckenbauer changed how soccer is played. He was a star for Germany and his club, Bayern Munich. He helped Germany finish second in the 1966 **World Cup**, and helped Bayern win three German league titles. His biggest mark came from how he played his position on defense.

From his position at the back, called **sweeper**, he began making long runs up the field. Defenders just didn't do that in those days! His speed and skill changed the position into a field-wide job. Opponents were just not set up to play against such a position and he dominated games. In 1974, Beckenbauer led Germany to the World Cup championship. In 1977, he moved to the United States to help the New York Cosmos win four league titles. He later became the first person to win a World Cup as player and coach, which he did with Germany in 1990.

In 2006, Beckenbauer was the head of a group that hosted the World Cup in Germany.

NUMBERS, NUMBERS

Beckenbauer was on the World Cup All-Star Team three times: 1966, 1970, and 1974.

6

JOHANN CRUYFF

NETHERLANDS

Like Beckenbauer, Johann Cruyff (KROYF) changed the sport by changing his position. He was a speedy, attacking center **forward**. But Ajax, his club team in the Netherlands, played something called "Total Football." In this system, every player can play every spot. They switch positions as needed. Cruyff was best up front, trying to score, but he could drop into **midfield** or to the **wing**.

Cruyff helped Ajax win six Dutch league titles and the European Cup three times. He brought Total Football to the national team, too. The Netherlands finished second in the World Cup in 1974 and 1978. After he retired, he became the coach of the famous Spanish team FC Barcelona. While he was in charge, they won 11 league or **cup** trophies.

Cruyff has a soccer move named for him. In the "Cruyff turn," a dribbler pulls the ball behind one foot with the other foot.

NUMBERS, NUMBERS

This great Dutch star was named European Footballer of the Year in 1971, 1973, and 1974.

ALFREDO DI STEFANO

Before Pelé, Cruyff, Maradona, and Ronaldo came along, this great offensive player was probably the best ever. Alfredo di Stefano grew up in Argentina and was one of the greatest **dribblers** of all time.

He started out with pro clubs in Argentina and helped River Plate win the South American championship in 1947. By the mid-1950s, he had moved to Europe to play in larger and tougher leagues. He was a star with Spain's Real (ray-AL) Madrid. Starting in 1956, that famous club won five straight European Cups. In each of the final games of those tournaments, di Stefano had at least one goal. In the 1960 final, he had a **hat trick**!

His greatest skill was his ability to do anything with the ball. His moves made him very hard to defend. Di Stefano set a high standard for the players who wanted to be called "the best in the world."

NUMBERS, NUMBERS

Teams with the Most European Cups (Now called the UEFA **Champions League**)

Real Madrid	12
AC Milan	7
Bayern Munich	5
FC Barcelona	5
Liverpool	5
Ajax	4

MARTA

BRAZIL

Can the No. 1 soccer superstar be a woman? Why not? Probably the best female player ever is Marta Viera da Silva, known simply as Marta.

She grew up in soccer-crazy Brazil. Though every boy in Brazil plays, most girls don't. Marta used to make her neighborhood boys crazy by beating them! She had to move to Sweden when she was 17 to play at a high level. She led her team there to four straight league titles. She later joined a league in the United States and became the MVP.

Starting in 2006, she was named the Women's World Player of the Year five times! Marta's greatest success came when playing for Brazil's national teams. She helped them win silver medals at the 2004 and 2008 Olympics. She has also scored the most goals ever in Women's World Cup games.

NUMBERS, NUMBERS

Through 2017, Marta had played 106 games for Brazil. In those games, she scored an amazing 105 goals!

LEV YASHIN

SOVIET UNION

With so much soccer talent in Europe, there's no end to great players. You had to be a pretty darned good 'keeper be named top player as a goalie! Lev Yashin did that in 1963!

Even all these years later, he is considered one of the best goalies of all time. He played 20 seasons with the club team Moscow Dynamo. They won the 1960 European Championship.

Yashin also played for his country, the Soviet Union. He helped them win the 1956 Olympic gold medal.

"The Black Panther" always wore all black clothes while playing. He was extremely athletic. He could leap very high and very far. He was also very smart in goal. How good? He posted more than 500 **shutouts** in his 800-plus games.

NUMBERS, NUMBERS

The penalty kick is the hardest shot to stop. It's just the kicker against the goalie from 12 yards out. In his long career, Yashin stopped an amazing 150 penalty shots.

Goalies control the penalty area. This is a rectangle in front of the goal. The top of the box is 18 yards from the goal line. Goalies can only use their hands on the ball inside this giant box.

ZINNEDINE ZIDANE

FRANCE

Zinnedine Zidane's soccer skill helped him escape a tough childhood in southern France. He joined a club in Italy and helped them win the Italian league twice. Zidane played midfield, controlling games with great passing and strong dribbling.

Zidane made his biggest mark at the 1998 World Cup, which was played in France. In the final match, against Brazil, Zidane scored the first two goals. He lifted the trophy as world champion after the match.

In 2002, Zidane moved to Spain to play for Real Madrid. He led them to the European club championship, scoring a key goal in the final. He also led France to second place in the 2006 World Cup before retiring. He later became a championship coach with Madrid.

NUMBERS, NUMBERS

Zidane's World Player of the Year Awards

1998

2000

2003

In 2004, the European pro clubs association turned 50. Fans voted for the top player in Europe during that time. The winner? Zidane!

DIEGO MARADONA

ARGENTINA

Short, tough, and determined: Diego Maradona didn't let anything or anyone get in his way. This talented forward from Argentina is on everyone's list of greatest players of all time. When Maradona was less than 10, he helped his team win 136 games in a row! That youth team was called *Las Cebollitas*, or Little Onions.

He started playing pro soccer in his home country with a club called Juniors and later helped another club win a league title. His ability to dribble around many players made him a star. Though he was not very tall, he was very strong. Even larger players could not stop him. He was signed by the famous FC Barcelona club in 1982 and scored nearly 40 goals in two seasons. His next move led to his best results. With Napoli in the Italian League, he became a two-time league champion and helped them win the Champions League.

Maradona held the World Cup trophy after he led his country to victory in 1986.

Maradona first played for Argentina's national team in 1977 at age 16, and later helped them reach the 1982 World Cup. In 1986, they won the whole thing, beating Germany in the final. In an earlier game, Maradona made headlines with two goals. On the first, it looked like he knocked the ball in with his hand against England but was not caught. On the second, he got the ball at midfield and dribbled past four English defenders to score. In 2002, that second goal was judged the best all-time in the World Cup. Argentina also finished as World Cup runner-up in 1990.

Sadly, Maradona had many problems with drugs and money. He was suspended from soccer twice after using drugs. He has gotten better in recent years and was the coach for Argentina's national team during the 2010 World Cup. His players could get lessons from him for life on and off the field.

NUMBERS, NUMBERS

In 91 games for Argentina from 1997 to 1994, Maradona scored 34 goals.

LIONEL MESSI

ARGENTINA

Sometimes, it seems like magic. Lionel Messi appears to do things with a soccer ball that just don't seem possible. He has used his dribbling magic and amazing ability to score to become a soccer legend. Known as "The Flea" for his small size and ability to move super-quickly, Messi is many fans' choice as the best player in the world.

Messi grew up in Argentina. He loved soccer and was very good at a young age. When he was 11, however, he found that he would have trouble growing. His body needed more of a certain chemical. To help him, the Spanish team FC Barcelona paid for some medical treatments. He began to grow and joined that team's youth academy. By the time he was 17, he was playing on the top Barcelona team.

NUMBERS, NUMBERS

In 2012, Messi scored 91 goals for club and country. That was a new world record for most goals in a year. He scored 79 for Barcelona in league and cup matches. He added a dozen in games played for Argentina.

La Liga is Spain's number-one soccer league. It was started in 1929. Messi is the all-time leading scorer in league history, with more than 350 goals through 2017.

By 2010, at age 22, he had 47 goals to lead the Spanish league. He has helped this great club win eight La Liga titles. Four times, FC Barcelona won the Champions League.

On goal after goal, Messi seems to create new ways to fool defenders. He can dribble past, through, or around them. He can score with either foot, from close up or long range. He helps teammates by sending them perfect passes when the defense closes down on him.

Messi also is a star for Argentina. In 2008, he led them to the gold medal at the Olympic Games in Beijing. In 2014, they finished second to Germany at the World Cup. Though he was disappointed not to win for his country, he did win the Golden Ball as the best player of that World Cup.

As one of the most dangerous players in the world, Messi will continue to be the focus of every defense he plays against.

CRISTIANO RONALDO

PORTUGAL

Is Cristiano Ronaldo the best player in the world? Just ask him. "I'm the best player in history," he said in 2017. "There's no player that is more complete than me."

He's not the only person to think so. In 2017, Ronaldo won his fifth World Player of the Year award. That tied Lionel Messi for most ever. In that season alone, Ronaldo led his club Real Madrid to five major championships in league and cup play.

He was born in Portugal and by the time he was 16, he was a superstar. He joined the English club Manchester United. When he was 17, he helped them win the league cup by scoring a hat trick in the final! In 2008, he had 31 goals to set a new team record.

Twice, Ronaldo sold an important trophy called the Golden Boot. The money from the sales was donated to charities. He also refuses to get any tattoos so that he can continue to donate blood regularly.

One of Ronaldo's biggest moments came in 2016. He led his small country to a surprise win in the European championship.

He moved to the Spanish team Real Madrid and led Spain's La Liga in scoring three straight seasons. Real Madrid also won three Champions League titles. With 114 goals through 2017, Ronaldo is the all-time leading Champions League scorer.

In 2016, Ronaldo helped create one of his greatest memories. Though Portugal is a small country, his talent had helped the national team improve by a lot. That year, he was the captain as his nation won its first European Championship.

Ronaldo is amazingly fit. He works hard in the gym and takes care of his body. He also takes care of other people. Ronaldo has donated millions to help children, including building a hospital and donating to disaster relief.

NUMBERS, NUMBERS

The Balon D'Or (Golden Ball): FIFA Player of the Year (Years Ronaldo was first or second)

Year	Winner	Runner-up
2017	Cristiano Ronaldo	Lionel Messi
2016	Cristiano Ronaldo	Lionel Messi
2015	Lionel Messi	Cristiano Ronaldo
2014	Cristiano Ronaldo	Lionel Messi
2013	Cristiano Ronaldo	Lionel Messi
2012	Lionel Messi	Cristiano Ronaldo
2011	Lionel Messi	Cristiano Ronaldo
2009	Lionel Messi	Cristiano Ronaldo
2008	Cristiano Ronaldo	Lionel Messi
2007	Kaká	Cristiano Ronaldo

PELÉ

BRAZIL

His first ball was made of rags. His first field was a dusty street. He didn't own soccer shoes until he was nine years old. From that tough start, Pelé became one of the greatest players ever. For a while, he was probably the most famous person in the world, period!

Pelé was born Edson Arantes do Nascimento in Brazil. He got the nickname Pelé when he was six or seven, but no one really knows where it came from or what it means! He started playing with his friends in the neighborhood. His first coach was his father, Dondinho, who was a fine pro player himself.

Pelé excelled in his small town, but soon the clubs in the big Brazilian cities recruited him. He joined a team in São Paulo called Santos. By the time he was 17, he was helping that team win league titles. In 1958, he made the Brazilian national team.

Pelé and Diego Maradona were named the Players of the Century in 2000. Maradona won the fans' poll on the Internet. Pelé was given the award by a panel of experts. He was named the Athlete of the Century by the International Olympic Committee.

The team traveled to Sweden to play in the World Cup. The teenager became a huge sensation. He helped Brazil win its first world championship.

Over the coming decades, Pelé kept topping himself. He helped Brazil win two more World Cups (1962 and 1970). He led Santos to league and South American titles. He became the first modern player to score 1,000 career goals.

By the mid-1970s, he had retired from Brazil's national team. He still wanted to play and help his sport. He was given a huge contract to move to the United States to join the Cosmos of the new North American Soccer League. He teamed with other world stars to put soccer on the map in the U.S. After he finally hung up his cleats, he became minister for sport in Brazil.

Today, Pelé is a goodwill ambassador for the United Nations and remains the most famous soccer player of all time.

NUMBERS, NUMBERS

All-Time World Cup Goals

Mirsolav Klose, Germany	16
Ronaldo, Brazil	15
Gerd Müller, Germany	14
Just Fontaine, France	13
Pelé	12

YOUR TOP TEN!

In this book, we listed our Top 10 in no particular order. We gave you some facts and information about each player. Now it's your turn to put the players in order. Find a pen and paper. Now make your own list! Who should be the No. 1 soccer superstar of all time? How about your other nine choices? Would they be the same players? Would they be in the same order as they are in this book? Are any players missing from this book? Who would you include? In this case, do you just list them in order of how many goals they scored? Or World Cups they won? It's your call!

Remember, there are no wrong answers. Every fan might have different choices in a different order. Every fan should be able to back up their choices, though. If you need more information, go online and learn. Or find other books about these great players. Then discuss the choices with your friends!

THINK ABOUT THIS . . .

Here are some things to think about when making your own Top 10 list:

• How did each player help his team or his country win?

• How important were the goals the player scored?

• Did the player help change the game at all?

• What were the player's different skills?

• Who would you want to take a championship-winning shot?

• Which is more important—big stats or championships?

SPORTS GLOSSARY

Champions League (CHAMP-ee-unz LEEG) sponsored by UEFA, which runs European soccer, this annual tournament matches the top teams from pro leagues on that continent

cup (KUPP) in soccer, a tournament among a small group of teams played over a short period of time

dribbler (DRIBB-ler) a soccer player who can use small touches on the ball to move past or around opponents

forward (FORE-wurd) a soccer position that plays toward the front of an offense and focuses on scoring

hat trick (HAT TRIK) scoring three goals in one game

midfield (MIDD-feeld) the area of the field closest to the center

shutout (SHUT-owt) a game in which one team does not allow a goal to the other team

sweeper (SWEEP-er) a soccer position that plays at the central back of the formation and focuses on defense

wing (WING) the parts of the field closest to the outside edges

World Cup (WURLD KUPP) the international championship for national soccer teams, played every four years

FIND OUT MORE

IN THE LIBRARY

Buckley, James Jr. *Who Is Pelé?* New York, NY:
Penguin/Grosset & Dunlap, 2018.

Hurley, Michael. *World Cup Heroes.* Seattle, WA: Raintree, 2015.

Kortemeier, Todd. *Superstars of World Soccer.*
Mankato, MN: Amicus Ink, 2017.

ON THE WEB

Visit our Web site for links about Top 10 soccer
superstars: **childsworld.com/links**

*Note to Parents, Teachers, and Librarians: We routinely verify our Web links to make
sure they are safe and active sites. So encourage your readers to check them out!*

INDEX

Ajax, 7
Argentina, 8, 12, 13
Bayern Munich, 6
Beckenbauer, Franz, 6
Brazil, 9, 18, 19
Champions League, 8, 17
Cruyff, Johann, 7
di Stefano, Alfredo, 8
England, 15, 16
FC Barcelona, 7, 12, 14
France, 11
Germany, 6, 15
Manchester United, 16, 17
Maradona, Diego, 12-13
Marta, 9
Messi, Lionel, 14-15, 17
Moscow Dynamo, 10
Napoli, 12

Netherlands, 7
New York Cosmos, 6, 19
North American Soccer League, 19
Olympics, 10, 15
Pelé, 4, 18-19
Portugal, 16, 17
Real Madrid, 8, 11, 17
River Plate, 8
Ronaldo, Cristiano, 5, 16-17
Santos, 18
Soviet Union, 10
Spain, 8, 10, 11, 14, 17
Sweden, 19
Women's World Cup, 9
World Cup, 6, 7, 11, 13, 15, 19
Yashin, Lev, 10
Zidane, Zinnedine, 11

ABOUT THE AUTHOR

K. C. Kelley has written dozens of books for young readers on everything from sports to nature to history. He wrote two different biographies of Pelé! He lives with his family in Santa Barbara, California.